U0100304

大展好書　好書大展
品嚐好書　冠群可期

大展好書　好書大展
品嘗好書　冠群可期

彩色圖解
太極武術
23

嫡傳楊家太極刀

13式

Authentic yangfamily tai chi sabre

13form

中國武術八段

傅聲遠 著

大展出版社有限公司

國家圖書館出版品預行編目資料

嫡傳楊家太極刀 13 式＝Authentic yangfamily tai chi sabre　傅聲遠　著
——初版，——臺北市，大展，2008〔民 97.10〕
　　面；21 公分 ——（彩色圖解太極武術；23）
ISBN　978－957－468－641－4（平裝）
1. 器械武術
528.974　　　　　　　　　　　　97015009

嫡傳楊家太極刀 13 式　　ISBN 978－957－468－641－4

著　　　者／傅　聲　遠
責任編輯／佟　　　暉
發 行 人／蔡　森　明
出 版 者／大展出版社有限公司
社　　　址／台北市北投區（石牌）致遠一路 2 段 12 巷 1 號
電　　　話／（02）28236031・28236033・28233123
傳　　　眞／（02）28272069
郵政劃撥／01669551
網　　　址／www.dah-jaan.com.tw
E - mail／service@dah-jaan.com.tw
登 記 證／局版臺業字第 2171 號
承 印 者／嶪聖彩色印刷有限公司
裝　　　訂／建鑫裝訂有限公司
排 版 者／弘益電腦排版有限公司
授 權 者／北京體育大學出版社
初版 1 刷／2008 年（民 97 年）10 月
定　　　價／220 元

楊家太極拳祖師　楊祿禪
（1799 年～1872 年）
Master of Yang Style Taijiquan (shadow boxing)
Yang Lu Chan

楊鳳侯（祿禪公　長子）
Yang Feng Hou

楊班侯（祿禪公　次子）
Yang Ban Hou

楊健侯（祿禪公　三子）
Yang jian Hou

楊少侯（健侯公　長子）
Yang Shao Hou

楊澄甫（健侯公　三子）
Yang Cheng Fu

楊兆元（健侯公　次子）
Yang Zhao Yuan

楊兆林（鳳侯公　子）
Yang Zhao Lin

楊兆鵬（班侯公　子）
Yang Zhao Peng

傅鍾文（兆元公　外孫婿）
Fu Zhong Wen

傅宗元（鍾文公　胞弟）
Fu Zong Yuan

傅聲遠（傅鍾文之子）
中國武術八段
楊式太極拳親族傳人
世界永年太極拳聯盟主席

Fu Sheng Yuan
（The Son of Fu Zhong Wen）
Chinese Wushu level 8
Cognation descendant of
Yang Style Taijiquan

傅清泉（傅聲遠之子）
中國武術七段
楊式太極拳親族傳人
世界永年太極拳聯盟副主席

Fu Qing Quan
（The Son of Fu Sheng Yuan）
Chinese Wushu level 7
Cognation descendant of Yang
Style Taijiquan

楊澄甫老師與弟子傅鍾文
Master Yang Chengfu and disciple
Fu Zhongwen

楊澄甫老師與弟子傅鍾文在廣州
Master Yang Chengfu and disciple
Fu Zhongwen in Guangzhou

1932 年傅鍾文跟隨老師楊澄甫到廣州市政府教拳
Fu Zhongwen and his master Yang Chengfu taught Taijiquan at
Government of Guangzhou City in 1932

上海永年太極拳表演隊　Shanghai Yongnian Taijiquan show team

傅聲遠和師伯崔毅士（中）、牛春明（右）老師在上海
Fu Shengyuan and his senior master Cui Yishi, master Niu Chunming at Shanghai

傅鍾文　Fu Zhong Wen

傅鍾文與傅聲遠推手
Tuishou between Fu Zhongwen and Fu Shengyuan

傅聲遠傅鍾文父子在香港
**Father Fu Zhongwen and son
Fu Shengyuan at Hong Kong**

傅氏三代在楊祿禪故居練拳
**Three Fu generations practice Taijiquan
at former residence of Yang Luchan**

傅聲遠被授予中國武術八段
FU Shengyuan is awarded Chinese Wushu level 8

澳大利亞總理霍克親切會見傅氏父子
Australian Prime Minister Mr. Bob Hawk gave an
interview to father and son of Fu

中華全國體育總會顧問徐才與傅聲遠合影
Group photo of Xu Cai, adviser of Chinese Sport
Association, and Fu Shengyuan

傅聲遠
Fu Sheng Yuan

傅公鍾文銅像
Bronze of Master Fu Zhongwen's Memorial Temple

傅公紀念祠大殿
Palatial Hall of Master Fu Zhongwen's Memorial Temple

傅公紀念祠牌坊
Memorial Archway of Master Fu Zhongwen's Memorial Temple

傅鍾文墓園 **Fu Zhongwen's Cemetery**

傅聲遠和西班牙政府官員合影
Group photo of Fu Shengyuan
and officer of Spanish

傅聲遠和西班牙學生
Fu shengyuan and
Spain students

傅聲遠和葡萄牙學生
Fu Shengyuan and
Portugal students

傅聲遠和泰國學生
Fu Shengyuan and his students in Thailand

傅聲遠和德國學生
FU Shengyuan and his
students in Germany

傅聲遠和美國學生
Fu Shengyuan and his
students in America

傅聲遠和英國學生
Fu Shengyuan and his
students in England

15

傅聲遠和智利學生
Fu Shengyuan and his students in Chile

傅聲遠和阿根廷學生
Fu Shengyuan and his students in Argentina

目　錄

高歌武術文化

徐　才

　　12年前，聲遠先生所著《嫡傳永年楊式太極拳》面市時，我曾於他寫過一篇短序《將武術獻給世界》以示祝賀。兩年前國際武術聯合會隨著武術在世界蓬勃發展之勢，決定每年5月爲「世界太極拳月」。今年在這個「世界太極拳月」裡，聲遠先生傳出喜訊，他又有幾本新書即將付梓，並再邀我爲之作序。我深爲這位移民海外的中華赤子之心所感動，所以接受了這項囑托。

　　我首先要向已是76歲高齡的聲選先生致敬：您眞老當益壯，老有所爲。從您的作爲又能看到您敎子有方，代代相傳祖業的心路。眞是上天不負苦心人。傅鍾文、傅聲遠、傅清泉太極世家三代人，定當一代勝似一代。

　　20年前，聲遠先生懷著把太極拳弘揚海外的虔誠之心移民澳洲。時間催人老，也催人的事業興。聲遠到了澳洲不顧年齡增長奮力進取，把太極拳這個中華武術的品牌在四十多個國家傳播得風風火火，他以澳洲爲立足點，每年敎遊四方。這正如美國著名的未來學家奈斯比特（John Naisbitt）在《亞洲大趨勢》書中所說：「西方正在學習適應東方化，而澳洲則首當其衝。」聲遠先生在海外傳拳授拳，就像他的父親傅鍾文大師那樣，不只是傳技而且傳理，還要傳德。這「三傳」是聲遠先生執敎之道，也是他爲人師品。我衷心祝願海內外熱心傳播中華武術的朋友，在「三傳」上狠下功夫，努力把中華武技、武理、武德廣泛撒播人世間。

　　聲遠先生在海外授拳創業，20年可謂成績斐然。這些年他勇於探索，勤於筆耕，以圖書和影帶形式向海內外習武者貢獻了太極拳的文化財富。在多元化的當今世界，不同文化的交流與交融是個大趨勢。不久前我從報紙上讀到一篇文章說：「與中國對外貿易『出超』相比，中國的對外文化交流和傳播則是嚴重『入超』，存在『文化赤字』。」這個論斷引起我強烈共鳴。是啊！中國是具有五千年歷史的文明古國，有著十分豐富的文化遺產，如今中國人民又在創造著嶄新的文化財富。爲什麼在文化「出口」方面我們處在一種弱勢狀態呢？這恐怕與我們對固有的文化強勢認識不足，對人類文化的互相凝聚，彼此滲透認識不足有關。

　　這裡說一個至今仍然能鼓舞國人奮力傳播中華文化的一位先輩人士，他就是清末在西方世界彌漫著歧視中國、歧視中華文化的氛圍下，率先以流暢的法文撰寫《中國人自畫像》、《中國人的快樂》、《中國戲劇》等書，向世界介紹中國和中華文化的陳季同。陳季同是福建人，他與同屬閩籍的辜鴻銘、林語堂是近代中國人用西文向世界介紹中國和中華文化的「福建三傑」。他們的作爲對當今盛世中國的文人武士具有莫大的啟示意義。可喜的是在中華武術走向世界的潮流中，已經出現一批以精湛的拳術和深情的筆墨向世界展示武術風采的專家，聲遠先生就是其中之一。我深切期望海內外武術家攜手高歌武術文化，造福於人類的健康、益智、修性，共創和諧社會和和諧世界！

2006 年 5 月於北京

Loudly Singing Wushu Culture

Xu Cai

Twelve years ago, when Fu Shengyuan's Exercise Method of Direct-Line Yang Style Taijiquan published, I have written a short preface "Consecrate Wushu to the World" for congratulating. Two years ago, Along with the rapid development of Wushu in the world, International Wushu Association decided to choose May each year as "World Taijiquan Month". This year, in this world Taijiquan Month, I got good news from Mr. Fu Shengyuan that the will publish some new books, and I was invited to write preface for his books. I was touched by his utter purity, thus received the entruse.

First, I will pay my respects to Mr. Fu Shengyuan who is already in 76 advanced age; you are indeed hale and hearty in old age. From your deeds, we found out you inherited your father's career, and gained achievements step by step, we found out you educated your son in right ways, descended undertaking of ancestors generation by generation. The three Taijiquan generations of Fu Zhongwen, Fu Shengyuan and Fu Qingquan is getting better generation after generation.

20 years ago, with sincere desire of developing Taijiquan to overseas, Mr. Fu Shengyuan migrated to Australia. Time elapse quickly, regardless the increasing age, Fu Shengyuan has transmitted Taijiquan over 40 countries. Based in Australia, he taught the disciples and students all over the world. As said in MEGATRENDS ASIA written by John Naisbitt that "The Western is trying to learn and adopt orientalization, and Australia is standing in the breach". Like his father master Fu Zhongwen, Mr Fu

Shengyuan not only teaches boxing, but also teach principle and moral, these are Fu Shengyuan's teaching way and his exemplary virtue also. I sincerely wish the friend who has his mind on transmit Chinese Wushu overseas, follows Mr. Fu Shengyuan's step, spread technique, principle and moral of Chinese Wushu all over the world.

Mr. Fu Shengyuan taught Taijiquan at overseas in the 20 years, and received brilliant achievements. He is brave in explore, diligent in writing, contributed valuable culture of Taijiquan to overseas Wushu exerciser in the forms of book and video tape. In the modern world, communication and blend of different cultures is a trend. Not long ago, I have read an article from newspaper that "Compare with'exceeding export'of Chinese foreign trade, Chinese culture communication and transmit is seriously 'exceeding import', there has Culture Deficit". I am sympathetic response on this judgment, yes! China is a cultural country with 5 thousand years'history, we have abundant cultural heritage, and now Chinese people is creating new culture fortune, but why we are in weak condition in culture superiority, less understanding on mutual agglomeration and mutual penetration of human cultures. Hereof, I will mentioned an ancestor–Chen Jitong. In the last stage of Qing Dynasty, under the atmosphere of Western world discriminate against China and Chinese culture, he wrote Chinese Self-portrait, Chinese Happiness, China Opera and other books in fluent France, Cheng Jitong is a native of Fujian, together with Gu Hongming and Lin Yutang, they were called as "Three Talents of Fujian" for they all introduced China and Chinese culture to the world in foreign languages. Their action gives well enlightenment to modern Wushu exerciser. Fortunately, in the trend of China Wushu develop to the world, a batch of experts is exhibiting graceful bearing of Chinese Wushu in their consummate Taijiquan technique and soulful writing, Mr. Fu Shengyuan is one of them. I sincerely hope Wushu experts in home and abroad can hand in hand to loudly singing Wushu culture, bring benefit to people' s health, mentality and temperament; create harmonious society and harmonious world together!

May 2006 in Beijing

陳微明爲永年太極拳社成立 10 週年賀詞

A Message to Commemorate the 10th Anniversary of the Yong Nian Tai Chi Association

陳微明
（ Chen Wei Ming ）

Mr. Fu Zhong Wen of Yong Nian has received the teaching and guidance from his relative, Mr. Yang Cheng Fu. Mr. Fu has learnt accurately to a very high standard, and has made no alterations, which is why people say that his Tai Chi is authentic.

Mr. Fu founded the Yong Nian Tai Chi Association（in 1944）, and has spread the art to the public for no charge. Ten Years have now passed since the founding of the Association, and I would like to say a few words to commemorate the occasion, When it comes to continuing the legacy of Yang Style Tai Chi, who else is there to compare with Fu Zhong Wen?

Chen Wei Ming was the first tuti（disciple）of the Great Master Yang Cheng Fu. He was a well known scholar, and he was responsible for his, teacher going to shanghai. Different from a student, a tuti（disciple）is accepted into the Yang family through formal ceremony, and is entitled to receive the full transmisson of the art. Disciple in this context has no religious connotation.

傅君鍾文永年 楊澄甫師之晚戚得

師之傳授規矩準繩絲毫不爽故人

稱為太極拳之正宗劍蔣永年太極

孝社教授學者不取報酬成就甚眾

今屆十載屬余書數語以為紀念爰

揚先大舍 鍾文其誰耶 陳徽明

傅鍾文題永年太極拳社社訓

The Yong Family Tai Chi Chuan Motto

Master Fu Sheng Yuan emphasizes the importance of the four principles of Zhin, Hen, Li, Zhen in the development of Tai Chi Chuan.

'Zhin' – Diligence

Hard work and effort is a prerequisite for skilled development. Daily practice on a regular basis will ultimately be rewarded by beneficial results.

'Hen' – Perseverance

It is important that a long enduring sense of purpose should be cultivated. A sense of purpose combined with regular daily practice serve to achieve that purpose.

'Li' – Respect

Respect for your master, teacher and fellow man is paramount. Deal with others taking into consideratioin their backgrounds and in the light of their expectctions. Mutual respect serves to enhance a sense of community in a society where individuals must treat each other with respect.

'Zhen' – Sincerity

Sincerity in attitude or motivation is a pre-requisite for learning Tai Chi Quan. In order to achieve, a genuine resolve to pursue your goal must exist. Deal with others sincerely if you wish them to reciprocate. Maintain sincerity in the fore of your dealings with others and you will achieve a smooth flow in relationships.

勤恒禮誠

傅鍾文

一九九年元月

Calligraphy by Grandmaster Fu Zhong Wen

太極拳說十要
Yang Cheng Fu's Ten Important Points For Practic

楊澄甫

一、虛靈頂勁
Hold the Head straight with Ease

頂勁者，頭容正直，神貫於頂也。不可用力，用力則項強，氣血不能流通，須有虛靈自然之意。非有虛靈頂勁，則精神不能提起也。

The head should be erect in order for the spirit to rise. If force is used, the back of the neck will be stiff, and the circulation of blood and chi will be impeded. There should be a natural, light and sensitive feel-ing. If not, the spirit will be unable to rise up.

In order to achieve the above, it is important that the neck is held straight, but very relaxed and alive. Keep your mouth natural with the tougue touching the upper palate. Avoid clenching your teeth or gazing out with an angry look. Keep your sacrum straight and slightly tucked under. If not, your spine will be affected, and your spirit will not be able to rise.

二、含胸拔背
Sink the Chest and Raise the Back

含胸者，胸略內含，使氣沉於丹田也。胸忌挺出，挺出則氣擁胸際，上重下輕，腳跟易於浮起。拔背者，氣貼於背也，能含胸則自能拔背，能拔背則能力由脊發，所向無敵也。

There should be a slight drawing in of the chest which allows the chi to sind to the Dan Tian. Avoid protruding the chest as this will cause the chi to rise which will lead to top heaviness, and the soles of the feet to float.

Raising the back means that the chi adheres to the back. If you can sink your chest, your back will naturally rise. If you can raise your back, your power will come from your spine enabling you to overcome any Opponent.

Sink the chest and raise the back are similar to when a cat is in readiness to launch an attack on its prey.

三、鬆　腰
Relax the Waist

腰為一身之主宰，能鬆腰然後兩足有力，下盤穩固，虛實變化皆由腰轉動，故曰：「命意源頭在腰隙。」有不得力必於腰腿求之也。

The waist is the commander of the body. If the waist is relaxed and loosened, the foundation, that is, your legs will be stable enabling you to issue power. Changes in solid and empty derive from the moving of the waist. It is said that「the waist is the well spring of your vital energy」. If you lack power in your movements, look for the weakness in your waist and legs.

四、分虛實
Distinguishing Solid and Empty

太極拳術，以分虛實為第一義，如全身皆坐在右腿，則右腿為實，左腿為虛；全身皆坐在左腿，則左腿為實，右腿為虛。虛實能分，而後轉動輕靈，毫不費力；如不能分，則邁步重滯，自立不穩，而易為人所牽動。

Distinguishing principle of Tai Chi. If your body centre rests in your right leg, then your right leg is solid, and your left leg is empty. If your body centre rests in your left leg, then your left leg is solid, and your right leg is empty. When you can clearly make this distinction, your movements will be light, agile, and effortless. If not, your steps will be heavy and chumsy, and you are easily unbalanced, due to the instability of your stance.

The philosophy of Yin Yang is the underlying principle of change in stepping.

五、沉肩墜肘
Sink the Shoulders and Elbows

沉肩者，肩鬆開下垂也。若不能鬆垂，兩肩端起，則氣亦隨之而上，全身皆不得力矣。墜肘者，肘往下鬆墜之意，肘若懸起，則肩不能沉，放人不遠，近於外家之斷勁矣。

The shoulders should relax and hang downwards. If the shoulders are raised, then the chi rises, and the whole body cannot summon up its power.

The elbows must relax and point downwardsl. If the elbows are raised, the shoulders will become tense inhibiting your ability to discharge you opponent to any great distance. Raising the elbows or shoulders is similar to breaking the jin which occurs in the external martial art systems.

六、用意不用力
Use the Mind and not Brute Force

太極拳論云：此全是用意不用力。練太極拳全身鬆開，不使有分毫之拙勁，以留滯於筋骨血脈之間以自縛束，然後能輕靈變化，圓轉自如。或疑不用力何以能長力？

蓋人身之有經絡，如地之有溝洫，溝洫不塞而水行，經絡不閉則氣通。如渾身僵勁滿經絡，氣血停滯，轉動不

靈，牽一髮而全身動矣。若不用力而用意，意之所至，氣即至焉，如是氣血流注，日日貫輸，周流全身，無時停滯。久久練習，則得真正內勁，即太極拳論中所云：「極柔軟，然後極堅剛也。」

太極拳功夫純熟之人，臂膊如綿裹鐵，分量極沉；練外家拳者，用力則顯有力，不用力時，則甚輕浮，可見其力乃外勁浮面之勁也。不用意而用力，最易引動，不足尚也。

　　According to the Tai Chi Classics, you use the mind and not brute force, In practice, your whole body is relaxed; not even using an ounce of brute force. If you employ brute force, you restrict the flow of energy through your sinews, bones and blood vessels. This will inhibit your freedom of movement preventing you from achieving agility, sensitivity, aliveness, circularity, and naturalness.

　　「How can you have power without using brute force?」 By making use of the meridians in the body. {Meridians are a network of pathways which transport chi throughout the body. They connect the superficial, interior, upper and lower portions of the human body, making the body an organic whole. } The meridians are similar to the rivers and streams of the earth. If the rivers are open, then the water flows freely. If the meridians are open, then the chi flows. If the meridians are blocked as a result of using stiff force, then the circulation of chi and blood becomes sluggish. Hence, your movements will not be nimble, and even if a hair is pulled, your whole body will be in a state of disorder.

　　Although your abdomen is full and alive, there is no force being used. For the chi to sink down to the Dan Tian slowly and naturally, the mind needs to be relaxed. By deeply relaxing while preforming your Tai Chi movements, your chi will move freely to every part of your body.

This will benefit the body greatly. On the other hand, if you tense your mind and forcefully try to move your chi, or use unnatural methods to circulate the chi, is if more than likely that blockages will occur which are harmful to your health.

When you are able to use your mind and not brute force, then wherever your mind goes, your chi follows. After a long period of diligent practic and chi circulating freely everyday, you develop jin {an internal power which is different form hard force}. This is what the Tai Chi Classice means by 「from true softness comes true hardness」. The arms of one who has Tai Chi kung fu will feel extremely heavy; like steel wrapped in cotton. People who practise external martial art systems look strong when they exert hard force. However, when they are not bringing their hard force into use, they are light and floating. You can see that this merely a superficial kind of strength. Instead of using the mind, they use brute force, Which makes them easy to manipulate. Hence not worthy of praise.

七、上下相隨
Coordinate your Upper and Lower Body

上下相隨者，即太極拳論中所云：「其根在腳，發於腿，主宰於腰，形於手指，由腳而腿而腰，總須完整一氣也。」手動、腰動、足動、眼神亦隨之動，如是方可謂之上下相隨，有一不動，即散亂也。

According to the Tai Chi Classics, 「the root is in the feet; issued through the legs; controlled by the waist; and expressed through the fingers. From the feet through the legs to the waist forms one harmonious chi」. When the hands, waist, and feet move, your gaze needs to follow in unison. This is what in meant by harmony of the upper and lower body. If one part of the body is not in concordance with the rest, it will result in chaos.

When you first learn Tai Chi, your movements are larger and more open than those of a seasoned practitioner. The larger movements ensure that you waist and legs are moving in concordance, and all parts of the body are in harmony.

八、內外相合
Unify your Internal and External

太極拳所練在神，故云：「神為主帥，身為軀使。」精神能提得起，自然舉動輕靈。架子不外虛實開合。所謂開者，不但手足開，心意也與之俱開，所謂合者，不但手足合，心意亦於之俱合，能內外合為一氣，則渾然無間矣。

Tal Chi trains the spirit. It is said that「the spirit is the leader, and the body follows its command」. If you can lift your spirit, then your movements will naturally be agile and alive. Postures are nothing more than solid and empty, opening and closing. Opening does not just involve the hands and feet, but they must work in concordance with the opening of the heart/mind. Closing does not just concern the hands and feet, but they should coordinate with the closing of the heart/mind as well. When the internal and external are unified as one harmonious chi, then there are no gaps anywhere.

The heart/spirit is like a concealed sword. Form the outside, your practice has the appearance of being relaxed and comfortable, but on the inside, your heart/spirit is concentrated and sharp as a sword.

九、相連不斷
Continuity; no Stopping

外家拳術，其勁乃後天之拙勁，故有起有止，有續有斷，舊力已盡，新力未生，此時最易為人所乘。太極拳用意不用力，自始至終，綿綿不斷，周而復始，循環無窮。原論所謂「如長江大河，滔滔不絕」，又曰「運勁如抽絲」，皆言其貫串一氣也。

The external martial art systems employ brute force which is stiff and unnatural. This force stops and starts; moves in a jerky fashion. When the old force is finished before the new one has begun, this is the time when one is most vulnerable to attacks. In Tai Chi, you use the mind and not brute force. From the beginning to the end, the movements are continuous without stopping; like an endless circle. This is what the Classics means by 「a great river flowingcontinuously never ending」, or 「moving the jin like reeling silk from a cocoon」. The above conveys the idea of stringing the movements together into one harmonious chi.

If your movements stop and start, you will be easily taken advantage of by your opponent because you have exhausted your old strength, and the new power is not yet born.

十、動中求靜
Seek Serenity in Activity

外家拳術，以跳躍為能，用盡氣力，故練習之後，無

不喘氣者。太極拳以靜御動，雖動猶靜，故練架子愈慢愈好。慢則呼吸深長，氣沉丹田，自無血脈僨張之弊。學者細心體會，庶可得其意焉。

The external martial art systems consider leaping and crouching to be of value. They exhaust their energy and after practice, they are out of breath. Tai Chi uses serenity to counter activity. Even when you are moving, you remain tranquil. When practising the posturse, the slower you move, the better the result. Slowness enables your breath to become deep and long with the chi sinking to the Dan Tian. This will naturally prevent the pulse rate from elevating. Students of Tai Chi should think deeply on the above in order to grasp its meaning.

It is important to practise the movements slowly, so that you can understand the meaning within the movements. Practising slowly helps to regulate your breathing enabling your breath to become deep and long allowing your chi to sink to the Dan Tian. Practising in this manner also preventy the fault of top heaviness which is caused by the chi rising up.

-Narrated by Yang Cheng Fu-Recorded by Chen Wei Ming-Expanded upon by Fu Sheng Yuan.

楊式太極刀練習方法

一、練習太極刀的時候，「頭部」不可偏歪或俯仰，必須將下頜收進，頭向上直頂，好像有東西在頭上似的，但切忌由於頭向上頂、下頜收進而產生了硬頭強項之弊。因此，頭向上頂還要注意頸肌肉的放鬆，即所謂「頂頭懸」，所謂「虛領頂勁」。「目光」必須是向前直視，不要在運動中產生斜視的現象。「口」則自然合閉，「舌」向上捲舐上顎。「口」呼「鼻」吸任其自然。

二、練習太極刀的時候，「身軀」必須中正不倚，「脊樑」與「尾閭」必須直而不偏；但是這並不等於身軀僵直的絲毫沒有靈活之意，在運動過程中遇到動作變化的時候，必須注意含胸拔背、沉肩轉腰的變化，初學時節須注意，否則日久難改，必流於板滯，功夫雖深，難以得盡致用矣。

三、練習太極刀的時候，「兩臂」而且關節、肌肉均須放鬆，「肩」要向下鬆沉，「肘」要保持下垂，並始終屈成弧形，「掌」要微張，「手指」要伸而微屈。

四、練習太極刀的時候，「兩腿」必須分清虛實。身體重量移於左腿時，則左實，而右腳則虛點地面；反之則右實左虛。所謂虛，並非空虛之意，而是其勢仍然未斷，

存有伸縮變化的餘意在裏面；所謂實，也並非是用力過猛，用勁過分之意，而是充實而已。所以屈膝下蹲的時候，只要略蹲就可，如果屈膝成半蹲就有些用勁過分了，同時，半蹲容易使上身前傾，失去了中正之勢，違反了不倚不偏的要求。

五、練習太極刀的時候，「兩腳」的前進後退，必須是起落猶如貓行，起步要靈，落步要輕；遇到踢腳的時候，要使腳面繃平，腳尖朝前，但是也不要過分的繃直，要使腿腳的肌腱均都放鬆、慢慢地踢出。

六、練習太極刀的時候，必須保持「安靜」，使意識集中，將精神貫注到每個細小的動作中去，不要一面在練習，一面在考慮別的事情。否則，運動便成了隨便的活動，減低了鍛鍊的價值。

七、練習太極刀的時候，必須使「呼吸」保持自然，不要受動作的影響而阻礙了自然的正常呼吸。呼吸的方式，雖然太極刀與太極拳同樣講究「氣沉丹田」地深呼吸，但是，在初學的時候不必拘束於這一點上，只要運用一般的「膈式呼吸」（腹呼吸）就可，不要專意的做隔膜升降運動。否則，會弄得呼吸不自然，動作也不自然，呼吸與動作更難協調。

八、練習太極刀的時候，必須運用圓活之「勁力」，不要運用僵勁和拙力。所謂圓活之勁，即是在身軀四肢自

然活動或站立的情況下，使某些可能放鬆的肌肉和關節做到最大限度的鬆弛。但是，這種最大限度的鬆弛，卻並非等於體驗鬆懈和疲逗，而是以最低限度的力量來推動動作，也即是以肌肉的最低限度的緊張來支配骨骼。

九、練習太極刀的時候，必須使動作完整一氣、綿綿不斷。身軀和四肢的活動要上下相隨、協調一致，特別是刀法與手法、步伐的配合更應取得和諧、統一，所謂「一動無有不動」。切忌動手不動腳，動刀不動手的弊病。同時，還要使每個動作都前後貫串起來，使整套太極刀從起勢到結束形成為一個單一的動作，中間沒有停頓，沒有間斷；雖然有些地方需要微頓，但是這僅僅是說把動作微微放慢的意思，並不是稍作停止的意思。

十、練習太極刀的時候，宜慢不宜快。但慢並不等於遲鈍和過溫，因此在速度問題上，必須避免過溫和遲鈍的現象。同時還要保持從開始到結束的中間速度快慢均勻，不要忽快忽慢，快慢不勻。

楊式太極刀套路名稱

1. 七星跨虎交刀勢　　　2. 騰挪閃展意氣揚
3. 左顧右盼兩分張　　　4. 白鶴展翅五行掌
5. 風捲荷花葉內藏　　　6. 玉女穿梭八方勢
7. 三星開合自主張　　　8. 二起腳來打虎勢
9. 披身斜掛鴛鴦腳　　10. 順手推舟鞭作篙
11. 下勢三合自由招　　12. 左右分水龍門跳
13. 卞和攜石鳳還巢

Insturtion

1. Seven stars and riding tiger
2. Soaring, drawing apart, avoiding, expanding
3. Splitting
4. White crane spreads wings
5. The lotus hidden among the leaves as the wind blows
6. Fair lady working with shuttle in 8 directions
7. Displaying the sabre at will
8. Taming the tiger
9. Spreading the sabre
10. Whipping the sabre
11. Three horzontal movements of the sabre between chest and waist
12. Swaying the sabre to the left and right with a jump
13. Phonix returning to its perch

一、七星跨虎交刀勢（1-4圖）

一、七星跨虎交刀勢

1. 向南方，雙腳開步站立，雙臂在兩旁放鬆，左手拿刀，刀尖向上，刀背靠著手臂，刀刃朝前。

2. 左手轉向右面，身體重心落於右腳同時把左腿提起，而右手慢慢握成拳。

3. 左腿轉向正東，左腳趾朝向東北方，坐左腿而把右腳慢慢地往東前方放，同時身體轉向東面，而雙手於胸部往前，左手交叉於右手的腕部。

4. 右腿退一步而雙手往右並右拳打開成掌。

5. 重心放於右腳，提起左腿並把左腳趾朝向東面。同時把雙手打開（同跨虎勢）。

3

1 Seven stars and riding tiger

1. Stand with feet a shoulder–width apart facing south. Relax your arms by your sides, holding the sabre vertically with your left hand. The blunt edge of the blade rests in the crook of your left arm. The sharp edge faces south.

2. Move your left hand to the right and sit on your right leg. Simultaneously, raise your left leg hand . slowly make a fist with your right hand.

3. Step to the east with your left leg, left toe pointing north–east. Sit on your left leg, and place your right toe gently forward on the ground towards the east. Simultaneously, turn towards the east and advance your hands at chest level, crossing left over right at the wrist.

4. Step back with your right leg and withdraw your hands to the right opening your right fist into a palm.

4

5. Sit on your right leg, raise your left leg and place your left toe gently forward on the ground towards the east. Simul taneously, sepa– rate your hands (as in "riding tiger").

5　　　　　　　6

二、騰挪閃展意氣揚（5-12圖）

二、騰挪閃展意氣揚

1. 身體轉向右邊，在腰的高低處左手往右旋轉，而且把右手交叉於左手上，同時左腳提起。

2. 往東前方並做弓步，同時雙手把刀柄往左移。刀背靠於左手肋，刀刃往北，刀柄向東。

3. 提起右腿同時雙手打開至左右。用右手把刀向右轉劃弧形。

4. 重心於左腿而用右腿往東南成弓步。同時，移動刀至左下方，用左手碰右腕。

5. 重心放於右腿而提起左腳，同時把刀收回至右邊，刀刃向東齊於腰，左手隨著右手。

6. 左腳往前東面而變弓步，同時刀刺向東面把刀刃轉

7　　　　　8

向北面，並左手轉向北，手心向外，手指向上。左腳趾向
東。

　　7. 左腳跟轉讓左腳趾轉東北，重心放於左腿。提右腿
同時刀向左面逆時針方向轉動刀刃引導於外面。

　　8. 右腳往東前方並變成弓步，同時刀向順時針方向轉
動，刀刃引導於外面而左手在刀背處向前推。

　　9. 重心放於左腿而右腿往後退，同時收回刀放於右
邊，左手保持靠著刀面。

　　10. 提起左腿向前至弓步，同時刀向東前方引導刀刃而
用左手推向刀背，刀身向下至45度。

2　Soaring, drawing apart, avoiding, expanding

1. Turning to your right, sweep your left hand to the right at waist
level and place your right hand over your left hand. Raise your left leg

9   10

and step forward into a bow stance facing east. Simultaneously, sweep the hilt of the sabre to the left with both hands. The blunt edge of the blade rests in the crook of your left arm. The sharp edge faces north. The hilt points east.

2. Raise yourself on your left leg to stand on one leg. Simultaneously, separate your hands to the left and right, sweeping the sabre around to the right with your right hand.

3. Sit on your left leg and step into a bow tance towards the south-east with your right leg. Simultaneously, move the point of the sabre forwards and down to the left. Touch your right wrist with your left hand.

4. Sit on your right leg and raise your left leg. Simultaneously, withdraw the sabre to your right, its blade pointing east at waist level. Left hand follows the right hand closely in coordination.

5. Step forward into bow stance towards the east with your left leg. Simultane-ously stab with the sabre towards the east, turning its sharp

11   12

edge to face north. In coordination, sweep your left hand towards the north, palm out, and fingers up. Your left toe points east.

6. Turn your left toe to the north–east by pivoting on your left heel. Sit on your left leg and raise your right leg. Simul–taneously, circle the sabre up and down to your left, leading with the sharp edge.

7. Step forward into a bow stance with your right leg towards the east. Simultaneously, circle the sabre forward and up, leading with the sharp edge and pushing on the blunt edge of the blade with your left hand.

8. Sit on your left leg and step back with your right leg. Simulta–neously, withdraw the sabre to your right, keeping your left hand lightly on the flat of the blade.

9. Raise your left leg and step forward into a bow stance towards the east. Simultane–ously, advance the sabre to the east, leading with the sharp edge and pushing on the blunt edge with your left hand. The sabre points down at 45 degrees.

13

三、左顧右盼兩分張（13圖）

三、左顧右盼兩分張

1. 重心於左腿，左腳跟轉使左腳趾朝向南，同時左手往右手方向。

2. 把右腳放於左腳旁，重心放於右腳上提起左腳。同時打開雙手，把刀向西劈，眼望刀。

3　Splitting

1. Sitting on your left leg, turn your left toe to point south by pivoting on your left heel. Simultaneously, move your left hand towards your right hand.

2. Place your right foot next to your left, then raise yourself on your right leg to stand on one leg. Simultaneously, separate your hands, cutting down with the sabre towards the west. Look in the direction of the sabre.

14

四、白鶴展翅五行掌（14-15圖）

四、白鶴展翅五行掌

1. 重心於右腳，右手往腰位，同時把左手向右手移，刀刃旋轉向下。

2. 左腳進一步向東，左腳趾往東北方向，重心放於左腳而右腳往東成弓步。同時把刀刃逆時針方向由下往上至東方，同時左手由右向左做弧形，稍至後，手掌向外，手指向上。

3. 重心於左腳，提起右腳，同時刀逆轉至左面，刀刃向前。右腳往前右腳趾往東南，同時刀旋轉至右面，刀刃向前。左手隨著右手，刀向東於頭的位置，刀刃向上。

4. 重心於右腳，左腳往前至弓步向東方向。同時打開雙手，把手收回至頭的位置，而 手往東前方於肩齊刀向東於頭的部位，刀刃向上。

15

4 White crane spreads wings

1. Sit on your right leg and lower your right hand to waist level. Simultane–ously, move your left hand towards your right. The sabre points up semi–vertically.

2. Step towards the east with your left leg, left toe pointing north–east. Sit on your left leg and step into a bow stance with your right leg towards the east. Simultaneously, circle the sabre down and up towards the east, leading with the sharp edge. In coordina–tion, sweep your left hand around to the left and slightly back, palm out, fingers up.

3. Sit on your left leg and raise your right leg. Simultaneously, circle the sabre up and down to your left, leading with the sharp edge. Step forward with your right leg, right toe pointing south–east. Simul–tane–ously, circle the sabre up to your right, leading with the sharp

edge. Left hand follows the right closely in coordination. The sabre points east at head level with the sharp edge up.

4. Sit on your right leg and step forward with your left leg into a bow stance towards the east. Simultaneously, separate your hands, pulling the sabre back at head level, while advancing your left hand towards the east at shoulder level. The sabre points east at head level with the sharp edge up.

16

五、風捲荷花葉內藏（16圖）

五、風捲荷花葉內藏

1. 重心於左腳，左腳跟向右轉。同時旋轉刀從左肩處至右肩處。

2. 右腳放至左腳旁，右腳趾向西北方向，把左手掌的中心位放在刀柄根部，推刀向東南方，刀刃向上。

3. 右腳伸直，左腳隨之離地，同時刀刺向東北方向，轉刀刃往下，眼望刀。

5 The lotus hidden among the leaves as the wind blows

1. Sitting on your left leg, pivot to the right on your left heel. Simultaneously, circle the sabre over your left shoulder towards your right shoulder.

2. Place your right foot next to your left, right toe pointing north–west. Place the center of your left palm on the end of the hilt. The sabre points north–east with the sharp edge up.

3. Raise yourself on your right leg to stand on one leg. Simultaneously, stab with the sabre towards the north–east, turning the sharp edge down. The left hand assists by pushing on the end of the hilt and following through partway. Look in the direction of the sabre.

17　　　　　　　　　　　　18

六、玉女穿梭八方勢（17–29圖）

六、玉女穿梭八方勢

　　1. 重心於右腳，左腳往西南，左手移向西南（像單鞭），眼看左手方向。

　　2. 重心於左腳，右腳往前，右腳趾向西同時旋轉刀從左肩至右肩，左手收回至右肩處。

　　3. 重心於右腳，左腳向前至弓步，向西南方。同時刀從左肩向前劈至西南方同時左手往下至前再向上（就像太極拳的玉女穿梭）。刀向西南方至 45 度，刀刃向下。

　　4. 重心於右腳提左腳，同時左手向下，而把刀向前平推送出，刀背在左手臂背僅低於手肘，刀刃向前。

　　5. 左腳向前至弓步，向西南方，推刀向前。

　　6. 重心於左腳，左腳跟轉動至左腳趾向右，重心於左

腳，提右腳。

　　7. 右腳往東南方至弓步，同時刀往右方向而刀柄往下收回至腰。同時左掌往前（就像太極拳的轉身撇身錘）。刀向前至 45 度處，刀刃朝下。

　　8. 重心於左腳，提右腳向東出步。

　　9. 重心於右腳，而左腳向東北方向至弓步，同時刀刺向 45 度東北方向，刀刃轉左。同時左手往下向前再向上（就像太極拳的玉女穿梭）。

　　10. 重心於右腳，提左腳，同時把左手往下而刀背在左手臂背僅在肘下刀刃向前。

　　11. 左腳往前東南方至弓步，刀往前握。

　　12. 重心於左腳，左腳跟轉左腳趾往右，重心於左腳，提右腳。

　　13. 右腳往西北至弓步，同時把刀往右面回收至腰位，

21

22

同時左手移向前（就像太極拳的轉身蔽身錘）。刀往前45度，刀刃朝下。

14. 重心於右腳，左腳提起向西跨步。

15. 重心於右腳，左腳提起向西南至弓步同時用刀刺向西南45度方向，刀刃轉左，同時左手往下，再向前並向上（就像太極拳的玉女穿梭）。

16. 重心於右腳，提左腳同時左手往下把刀換成平位，刀背靠著左手臂在肘下刀刃向前。

17. 左腳往西南至弓步，刀向前推。

18. 重心於左腳，左腳跟轉動，左腳趾向右，重心於左腳，提右腳。

19. 左腳往東南至弓步，同時刀由左往右刀柄向下收回至腰。同時左手向前推（就像太極拳的轉身蔽身錘），刀向前45度，刀刃向下。

6 Fair lady working with shuttle in 8 directions

1. Sit on your right leg and step towards the south—west with your left leg. Move your left hand towards the south—west (as in 「ingle ship」). Look in the direction of your left hand.

2. Sit on your left leg and step forward with your right leg, right toe pointing west. Simultaneously, circle the sabre over your left shoulder towards your right shoulder. In coordination, withdraw your left hand towards your right shoulder.

3. Sit on your right leg and step forward with your left leg into a bow stance towards the south—west. Simultaneously, bring the sabre forward from your right shoulder and cut down towards the south—west. In coordinat—ion, move your left hand down, forward and up (as in 「air lady working with shuttle」). The sabre points south—west at 45 degrees with the sharp edge down.

4. Sit on your right leg and raise your left leg. Simultaneously,

25

drop your left hand, and move the sabre into a horizontal position, plac‐
ing its blunt edge on your left forearm just below the elbow. The sharp
edge faces forward.

5. Step forward into a bow stance towards west–south–west with
your left leg, pressing the sabre forward.

6. Sitting on your left leg, turn your left toe to the right by pivoting
on your left heel. Sit on your left leg and raise your right leg.

7. Step into a bow stance towards the south–east with your right
leg. Simul‐taneously, draw the sabre around to the right, pulling the
hilt back and down to below waist level. In coordination, move the left
palm forward (as in 「urn, sidle and punch」). The sabre points for‐
ward at 45 degrees with its sharp edge facing down.

8. Sit on your left leg, raise your right leg and step to the east.

9. Sit on your right leg and step into a bow stance towards the
north–east with your left leg. Simultaneously, stab 45 degrees up to‐
wards the north–east with the sabre, turning its sharp edge to the left.
In coordination, your left hand moves down, forward and up (as in 「air

lady working the shuttle」).

10. Sit on your right leg and raise your left leg. Simultaneously, drop your left hand, and move the sabre into a horizontal position, placing its blunt edge on your left forearm just below the elbow. The sharp edge faces forward.

11. Step into a bow stance towards east–north–east with your left leg, pressing the sabre forward.

12. Sitting on your left leg, turn your left toe to the right by pivoting on your left heel. Sit on your left leg and raise your right leg.

13. Step into a bow stance towards the north–west with your right leg. Simultaneously, draw the sabre around to your right, pulling the hilt back and down to below waist level. In coordination, move your left hand forward (as in 「urn, sidle and punch」). The sabre points forward at 45.degrees with the sharp edge down.

14. Sit on your left leg, raise your right leg and step to the west.

15. Sit on your right leg, raise your left leg and step into a bow stance towards the south–west. Simultaneously, stab 45 degrees up to-

28

29

wards the south−west with the sabre, turning its sharp edge to the eft. In coordination, your left hand moves down. Then forward and up (as in 「air lady working the shuttle」).

16. Sit on your right leg and raise your left leg. Simultaneously, drop your left hand, and move the sabre into a horizontal position, plac−ing its blunt edge on your left forearm just below the elbow. The sharp edge faces forward.

17. Step into a bow stance towards the west−south−west with your left leg, pressing the sabre forward.

18. Sitting on your left leg, turn your left toe to the right by pivot−ing on your left heel. Sit on your left leg and raise your right leg.

19. Step into a bow stance towards the south−east with your right leg. Simul−taneously, draw the sabre around to your right, pulling the hilt back and down to below waist level. In coordi−nation, move your left hand forward (as in 「urn, sidle and punch」). The sabre points forward at 45 degrees with its sharp edge down.

30　　　　　　　　　　31

七、三星開合自主張（30-33圖）

七、三星開合自主張

1. 重心於右腳，提左腳，向北成弓步，放鬆手臂稍分開。

2. 重心於左腳，左手掌放在刀柄根部，刀朝向東面，刀刃朝上，眼望刀。提右腳成獨立式，同時往東刺刀，刀刃朝上。

3. 左腳稍彈跳，微離地面；右腳著地，左腳趾往前放至東北方向，同時刀弧形環繞下切，往下（東北方向），刀刃朝下，用左手掌握，刀背向下。

32　　　　　　　　　　33

7　Displaying the sabre at will

1. Sit on your right leg, raise your left leg and step into a bow stance towards the north. Relax your arms, moving them apart slightly.

2. Sit on your left leg and place your left palm on the tip of the sabre hilt. The sabre points east with the sharp edge up. Look in the direction of the sabre.

3. Raise yourself on your left leg to stand balanced on one leg. Simultaneously, stab with the sabre to the east with its sharp edge up. In coordination, move your left hand in the opposite direction, palm out, fingers up. Look in the direction of the sabre.

4. Spring up on your left leg, land on your right leg, then place your left toe forward gently on the ground towards the north-east. Simultaneously, bring the sabre down towards the northeast, turning its sharp edge down, and pressing down on the blunt edge with the palm of your left hand.

34

八、二起腳來打虎勢（34-36 圖）

八、二起腳來打虎勢

1. 左腳向前踏半步，把刀轉到左手，刀背放在左手肘關節處。

2. 右腳朝東面踢，右手拍右腳背，同時左手往反方向。

3. 右腳放在左腳邊，重心落於右腳，提左腳。

4. 左腿往西北方做弓步，同時手劃弧形到左（就像太極拳的左打虎式），左手握刀柄齊於頭部，而刀背靠在左手臂肘處，右手變成拳齊於腰。

5. 重心落於左腿，轉左腳跟，左腳趾往後，重心移到右腿。提左腳往東南作弓步，同時雙手往右做弧形到右面（就像太極拳的右打虎式）。左手拿刀柄齊於腰，刀背靠左手臂肘，右手握拳齊於頭部。

35

8 Taming the tiger

1. Take a half–step forward with your left leg. Transfer the sabre to your left hand, resting the blunt edge in the crook of yor left arm.

2. Kick towards the east with your right leg and pat your right in-tep with your right hand. In coordination, your left hand moves in the opposite direction.

3. Place your right foot next to your left, sit on your right leg and raise your left leg.

4. Step into a bow stance towards the north–west with your left leg. Simultaneously, circle your hands to the left (as in 「aming the tiger to the left」). The left hand holds the hilt of the sabre at head level with the blunt edge resting in the crook of the left arm. The right hand forms

36

a fist at waist level.

5. Sitting on your left leg, turn your left toe to the right by pivoting on your left heel. Sit on your left leg, raise your right leg and step into a bow stance towards the south–east. Simultaneously, circle your hands to the right (as in 「aming the tiger to the right」). The left hand holds the hilt sabre at waist level with the blunt edge resting in the crook of the left arm. The right hand forms a fist at head level.

37

九、披身斜掛鴛鴦腳（37-38 圖）

九、披身斜掛鴛鴦腳

1. 重心於左腿，把右拳打開至掌，雙手交叉，左手在右手之上。

2. 右腿朝東面踢，同時右手往相同方向移動。

3. 把右腳和右手收回，把刀移到右手。

4. 刀往東平劈，同時左手往反方向移動，手掌朝外，手指向上，刀朝東方平面，刀刃朝下。

38

9　Spreading the sabre

1. Sit on your left leg and open your right fist into a palm. Cross your hands at the wrists, right under left.

2. Kick towards the east with your right leg, moving your right hand in the same direction.

3. Standing firm on one leg, withdraw your right foot and your right hand. Transfer the sabre to your right hand.

4. Cut down towards the east. In coordi-nation, your left hand moves in the opposite direction, palm out, fingers up. The sabre points horizontally to the east with the sharp edge down.

39

十、順水推舟鞭作篙（39-41 圖）

十、順水推舟鞭作篙

1. 身體轉右，放下右腳落地，右腳趾向南，同時刀往右旋轉至右肩，刀靠右肩，背部朝下。

2. 提左腳而繼續轉右方向南，繼續轉刀繞過頭至左肩，刀靠左肩背部朝下。

3. 右腳離地屈膝提起，而把左腳著地，左腳趾向西；繼續轉身往右，刀旋轉過頭至左肩，左手移至身前。

4. 重心於左腿，提右腿，同時右手持刀屈肘，將刀橫於身前，刀刃朝前。

10 Whipping the sabre

1. Turn to your right and put your right foot down, toe pointing

40   41

south. Simultane-ously, circle the sabre around to the right towards your right shoulder. The sabre points down behing your right shoulder.

2. Raise your left foot and continue turning to your right. Continue circling the sabre past the back of your head towards your left shoulder. The sabre points down behind your left shoulder.

3. Put your left foot down, toe pointing west. Keep turning to your right and circling the sabre past your left shoulder. Withdraw your left hand at waist level.

4. Sit on your left leg and raise your right leg. Simultaneously, draw the sabre around to the right at chest level. The blade is horizontal with its sharp edge facing forward.

5. Step forward with your right leg into a bow stance towards the northwest. Simultaneously, pull the sabre down to your right, while moving your left hand forward (as in 「urn, sidle and punch」).

42

十一、下勢三合自由招（42-44 圖）

十一、下勢三合自由招

1. 重心於左腿，提右腿往西作弓步，同時用雙手推刀往前方。刀平橫於身，刀刃向前，左手掌推刀背。

2. 重心於右腿，右腳跟轉右使腳趾成 45 度，重心於右腿，把左腳往西慢慢落地，同時刀刃橫掃至右後面，眼望刀。

3. 轉左腳跟使左腳趾朝 45 度方向，重心於左腿；右腿往西做弓步，同時刀刃橫掃於身前往西面，同時左手移動至左後面，手掌朝外，手指朝上。

43

11   Three horzontal movements of the sabre between chest and waist

1. Sit on your left leg, raise your right leg and step into a bow stance towards the west. Simultaneously,press the sabre forward using both hands. The blade is horizontal with the sharp edge forward. The left palm pushes on the blunt edge.

2. Sitting on your right leg, turn your right toe 45 degrees to the right by pivoting on your right heel. Sit on your right leg and place your left foot gently on the ground towards the west. Simulta--neously, sweep the sabre horizon–tally to the right and back, leading with the sharp edge. Look in the direction of the sabre.

71

44

3. Turn your left toe 45 degrees to the left by pivoting on your left heel. Sit on your left leg, and step forward with your right leg into a bow stance towards the west. Simultaneously, sweep the sabre horizontally to the west, leading with the sharp edge. In coordination, sweep your left hand out and back to the left, palm out, fingers up.

45

十二、左右分水龍門跳（45–48 圖）

十二、左右分水龍門跳

1. 提右腳成獨立式，同時刀刃逆時針旋轉至西南方，左手碰右手腕。

2. 重心於左腿，右腿往西北方向，右腳趾向北，重心於右腿。而左腿向西北至弓步。同時順時針旋轉刀至前方再繼續往後旋轉，眼望刀。

3. 提右腳作獨立式，同時刀刃順時針橫掃至前。左手碰右手，刀向平行西北方，刀刃朝上，眼望刀。

4. 左腿稍作屈膝，右腳開始落步同時，刀刃逆時針方向旋轉至前，收回左手至腰齊，重心於右腳，把左腳趾往前西北慢慢落地，再同時把刀收回配合左手向前推。刀向西北方稍向上，刀貼靠腰，刀刃朝下，眼向左手方向看。

46   47

12   Swaying the sabre to the left and right with a jump

1. Raise yourself on your left leg to stand on one leg. Simultaneously, circle the sword in an anticlockwise direction towards the south–west, leading with the sharp edge. The left hand touches the right wrist.

2. Sit on your left leg and step towards the north–west with your right leg, pointing your right toe north. Sit on your right leg and step forward into a bow stance with your left leg towards the north–west. Simultaneously, sweep the sbare anticlockwise to the front, then clockwise to the back, leading with the sharp edge. Look in the driection of the sabre.

3. Raise yourself on your left leg to stand on one leg. Simultaneously, sweep the sabre clockwise to the front, leading with the sharp

48

edge. The left hand touches the left forearm. The sabre points horizontally to the north–west with the sharp edge up. Look in the direction of
the sabre.

    4. Circle the sabre back in an anticlockwise direction.

    5. Spring up with your left leg and land on your right leg. Simulta-
neously, circle the sabre forward in an anticlockwise direction, leading
with the sharp edge. Withdraw the left hand at waist level.

    6. Sit on your right leg and touch your left toe gently forward on the
ground towards the north–west. Simutlancous–ly, pull the sbare back
while pushing your left hand forward in coordination. The sabre points
slightly up from waist level towards the north–west, with the sharp edge
down. Look in the direc–tion of your left hand.

49   50

十三、卞和攜石鳳還巢（49-54 圖）

十三、卞和攜石鳳還巢

1. 重心於右腿，提左腿，同時刀旋轉至頭後方至右肩，把左手收回至右肩，刀在右肩後朝下。

2. 左腿往西北做弓步，同時刀劈下向西北方向，配合使左手向下移至前向上（就像太極的玉女穿梭）刀向西北方，刀尖朝上 45 度刀刃朝下，眼望刀的方向。

3. 重心於左腿轉左腳跟，使左腳趾往右，把刀移到左手，刀背靠左手臂肘。

4. 右腿後退，右腳趾向東南方，重心於右腿，提左腿。腰轉右，把雙手轉右，左手慢慢握拳。

5. 把左腳趾朝東慢慢落地，右手向東前下方出拳，同時左手劃弧形由後至左面，刀背靠左手臂肘，眼望右拳方

51   52

向看。右腿慢慢起來，左腿放右腳旁至肩寬，人面朝南；
同時把拳打開變掌，把雙手收回至起勢動作同。

13 Phoenix returning to its perch

1. Sit on your right leg and raise your left leg. Simultaneously, circle the sabre behind your head towards your right shoulder. Withdraw your left hand towards your right shoulder. The sabre points down behind your right shoulder.

2. Step into a bow stance with your left leg towards the north-west. Simultaneously, cut down towards the north-west with the sabre. In down, forward and up (as in 「fair lady working shuttle」). The sabre points up at 45 degrees towards the north-west with the sharp edge down. Look in the direction of the sabre.

3. Sitting on your left leg, turn your left toe to the right by pivoting on your left heel. Transfer the sabre to your left hand. The blunt edge of the blade rests in the crook of your left arm.

53   54

4. Step back with your right leg, pointing the right toe towards the south-east. Sit on your right leg and raise your left leg. Turning your waist to the right, move both hands around to your right, while slowly forming a fist with your right hand.

5. Placing your left toe gently on the ground towards the east, punch forward and down towards the east with your right hand. In co-ordination, your left hand sweeps around to the left, with the blunt edge of the sabre resting in the crook of your left arm. Look in the direction of your right fist.

6. Raising on your right leg, place your left foot next to your right in the shoulder-width stance facing south. Simul-taneously, open your fist, and return your hands to the opening position.

Tai Chi Sabre Applications

A + B ready technique.

Holding the sabre face-to-face.

1）A：Step forward to cut B 挏 shoulder.

    B：Step to the side turning quickly, chopping inside A 挏 wrist

2）B：Step forward and thrust at A's stomach.

    A：Step back to cut the outside of B's wrist over the top of B 挏 sabre.

3）A：Step forward and thrust at B's waist.

    B：Move to the side and chop outwards at A's wrist.

4）B：Step toward A pushing the blade edge forward to cut A's throat.

    A：Push the sabre edge to cut B's wrist.

5）B：Cut down at A's leg from side on.

    A：Raise the leg and cut down at B'sswrist.

6）A + B：Embrace the sabre, lifting the leg.

跋 一

傳聲遠師父風塵僕僕馬不停蹄地在世界各地推廣嫡傳楊氏太極拳，百忙中不忘著書立說，近期內又將出版拳、劍、刀等系列著作，完整地保存了楊澄甫先師傳傳鍾文老師系的太極拳、械風格內容。這是師父繼《嫡傳楊式太極拳教練法》出版後再接再厲的嘔心之作。在這之前，師父已經出版多本中英文拳著及錄影帶、光碟等教材，暢銷世界各地，可謂著作等身。

由於他數十年如一日在國內外推廣傳統楊氏太極拳，功勞巨大，因此榮獲中國武協頒發的武術推廣獎，也獲得中國武術院頒發的武術段位八段。

師父9歲從永年到上海隨其父傳鍾文習練楊家太極拳，耳濡目染、勤勞苦學，全面繼承了楊澄甫先師太極拳晚期定型的85式楊氏太極拳架及器械。他早年跟隨父親傳鍾文在上海同濟大學、華工學院、財經學院及國內各地教拳。

1988年定居澳洲柏斯，並創立世界永年太極拳聯盟及傳聲遠國際太極學院。他以澳洲為大本營，向歐美及南洋一帶傳藝，桃李滿天下，將楊氏太極拳傳播到世界各地。傳鍾文太師是近代中國楊氏太極拳的代表人物之一，全面繼承了楊澄甫先師晚期定型的太極拳，經年累月，一絲不苟，被其師兄著名太極拳名家陳微明讚譽為太極拳正宗。

陳微明是楊澄甫先師器重的弟子，德高望重，影響深遠的博學之士，著有《太極拳術》等書，是研究楊氏太極拳的必讀著作。他在1954年上海永年太極拳社慶祝10周年紀

念時，親筆寫下這樣的贊語：「傅君鍾文永年楊澄甫師之晚戚，得師之傳授，規矩準繩絲毫不爽，故人稱太極拳之正宗——發揚光大，捨鍾文其誰子耶。」在武林慣例中，師弟能獲得師兄的公開贊許和勉勵是非常罕見的，也是一件不容易的事。因此傅鍾文太師傳承的太極拳風格，是楊氏太拳愛好者學習的典範。

楊澄甫先師晚期在《太極拳使用法》和《太極拳體用全書第一集》中刊登的拳照，渾厚圓滿，舒展大方，氣魄大，形象美，達到爐火純青的境界，是楊式太極拳的楷模，經典拳架。可惜的是，拳照中缺乏轉折過渡的動作。因此，習者莫不師從傅鍾文太師、傅聲遠大師、傅清泉師兄傳家三代尋求這些細膩重要的運作過程，以求合乎正宗。這是因爲在楊澄甫的弟子中，最相似楊澄甫定型的太極拳者，當推傅鍾文太師。

傅鍾文太師早年編著的《楊氏太極拳》、《楊氏太極刀》，被譯成多國文字，早已成爲楊氏太極拳的重要著作。1989 年由上海同濟大學出版的傅鍾文、傅聲遠編著《楊氏太極教練法》一書，出版後即洛陽紙貴。

1990 年傅聲遠師父編著的《嫡傳楊氏太極拳教練法》，用的是師兄清泉的拳照。清泉師兄有"太極少帥"之美譽，秉承家學，長期隨爺爺及父親身邊，親受教誨。曾在中國國內獲得楊式太極劍冠軍、中國武術七段，目前是少壯派的太極拳名師，學生遍布中國、日本、澳洲等地。該書已接二連三再版，仍供不應求。

師父傅聲遠 9 歲隨父練拳，苦下功夫，深受其父影響，他秉承家訓，在國內及海外走南闖北，應邀到世界各地授

拳。他虛懷若谷，不爭名利，教學認眞，在上海曾受聘於同濟大學、華工學院、財經學院、職工大學等高校教授太極拳。1986年他挾藝南來，先後在澳洲、泰國、新加坡、馬來西亞等國教授太極拳。定居澳洲柏斯後，他每年都風塵僕僕多次赴歐美四十多個國家授拳訪問，深受太極拳愛好者的歡迎，桃李滿天下，可謂是東南亞等國傳播楊式太極拳85式定型拳的第一人。如今傅聲遠師父的《嫡傳楊家太極拳》、《嫡傳楊家太極劍》、《嫡傳楊家太極刀》，即將出版，全面地展現了楊澄甫先師的拳、械體系，相信太極拳愛好者可以由傅師父的完整系列著作，得到啓發，登堂入室地直探楊公澄甫定型太極拳、械眞髓。

　　是爲跋

受業：黃建成

2006年6月23日馬來西亞光華日報　柔佛辦事處

　　註：作者爲馬來西亞中文報資深報人及文化人、馬來西亞柔佛新山永年太極拳學會會長、馬來西亞武術網和馬來西亞太極網絡站長。

Postscript I

Master Fu Shengyuan promotes Yang Style Taijiquan in the world without a stop, and writes books at the same time. Recently, the series books including boxing, sword and knife are on publish, which completely preserved, boxing and weapon contents of Master Fu Zhongwen (Yang Chengfu's disciples). This is another masterpiece after his publication of Exercise Method of Direct-Line Yang Style Taijiquan. Before that, master Fu has published many boxing writings, video tapes and CDs in Chinese and Engilsh, which sold briskly and easily all over the world.

For his persistent promotion on traditional Yang Style Taijiquan both in domestic and abroad for decades on end, he is granted Wushu Promotion Award by Chinese Wushu Association, and gained Wushu Level 8 from Chinese Wushu Academy. From Yongnian to Shanghai, Master Fu exercised Yang Style Taijiquan following his father Fu Zhongwen since 9 years old, through assiduously exercise, he completely inherited 85 FormYang Style Taijiquan and weapons from Master Yang Chengfu. In his early years, he followed his father Fu Zhongwen to taech Taijiquan at Shanghai Tongji University, Shanghai University of Economics and Finance, South China University of Technology and other domestic places.

The master settled down at Perth, Australia in 1988, and creatde World Yongnian Taijiquan Association and Fu Shengyuan International Taiji School. Based in Australia, he taught many disciples and students Taijiquan at Europe, USA and Southeast Asia, spread Taijiquan all over the World. Master Fu Zhongwen, Fu Shenguan's teacher and father, is one of representatives of Yang Style Taijiquan in modern times, has completely inherited definitized Taijiquan from master Yang Chengfu, and was highly praised by his senior fellow apprentice Chen Weiming, the famous Taijiquan expert, as orthodox Taijiquan. Chen Weiming is thought highly of by deceased teacher Yang Chengfu, is an erudite commendable person who has writings of Taijiquan and others. In 1954, Chen Weiming autographed the following words of praise: "Fu Zhongwen is satisfying purple of Yongnian Yang Chengfu, have proper behavior, and is known as orthodox Taijiquan. Fu Zhongwen will further develop and promote Taijiquan". In the Wulin convention, it is seldom that junior fellow apprentice is publicly praised by senior fellow apprentice. The style of Taijiquan from Fu Zhongwen is paragon to Yang Style Taijiquan lover. The photo of master yang Chengfu in Taijiquan Exercise Method and Entire Book on Taijiquan (No.1) shows his decent boxing posture, but it is a pity that there miss the transition posture in the photo. The person who know what's what all try to find the importnt orthodox postures from three generations of Fu Zhongwen, Fu Shengyuan and Fu Qingquan, this is because that in the Yang Chengfu's disciples, the most similar Taijiquan posture type should be Fu Zhongwen. The Yang Style Taijiquan and Yang Style Taijidao (taiji knife) which written by Fu Zhongwen at his early age has been branlated into many languages and be look as important writing for Yang Style Taijiquan. The Exercise Method of Yang Style Taijiquan, which written by Fu Zhongwen and Fu Shengyang, was published by Shanghai TongJi University Press in 1989. After the publication, the book was sold in overwhelming popularity. The book used boxing photo of Fu Zhongwen. But it is a pity that the paper quality of the book is not good. In 1990, Yongnian Yang Style Taijiquan (written by Fu Shengyuan) is published by Malaysia Yongnian Taijiquan Association. About 600 Master Fu Shengyuan's photo are used in the book, the book was already sold out, domestic lovers hasn't chance to get the book. Shanghai TongJi University published Exercise Method of Direct-Line Yang Style Taijiquan written by Fu's three generations in 2000, the book adopt Fu Qingquan's Boxing Picture. Fu Qingquan has good reputation of "junior commander in chief of Taijiquan". He followed his father and grandfather and received paternal teaching for long time, has gained champion of Yang Style Taijiquan (taiji sword), China Wushu Level 7, Now he is a famous Taijiquan master wit lots of disciples all over China, Japan, Australian, and other places. The book was republished for many times, but the damand still exceeds supply.

Master Fu Shengyuan practiced Taijiquan since 9 years old, deeply influenced by his father.He is extremely open-minded, stand aloof from the worldly affairs, and conscientiously teach Taijiquan at Tongji University, Shanghai University of Economics and Finance, South China University of Teachnology, College for Workers & Staff and other universities in Shanghai. In 1986, he went to south, taugh Taijiquan at Australia, Thailand, Singapore, Malaysia and other countries. After he teach Taijiquan each year, is popular with Taijiquan lovers. He can be No.1 who teach and transmit 85 Form Yang Style Taijiquan at Southeast Asia with student all over the world. At present, the 3 books of Proficiency in 28 Postures of Yang Style Taijiquan, Yang Style TaijiJian (taiji sword) , Yang Style Taijidao (taiji knife) , will be published in succession. These books will fully exhibit Taijiquan and weapons system of master Yang Chengfu. I believe the Taijiquan lovers will take a hint in studying the essence of Yang Chengfu Style Taijiquan and weapons through the complete series books. The Postscript is given hereby.

Student: Huang Jiancheng
Jun. 23, 2,
Note: the author is senior journalist and literator of Chinese newspaper in Malaysia, president of Johore Bahru Yongnian Taijiquan Association, Webmater of Malaysia Wushu website and Malaysia Taiji website. 006 at Johore Office, Kwong Wah Yit Poh & Penag Sin Poe

跋 二

　　吾師傅聲遠是一代太極宗師傅公鍾文之獨子，楊家太極拳親族傳人，中國武術八段，世界永年太極拳聯盟主席、澳洲傅聲遠國際太極拳學院主席。1931年生於河北永年廣府，9歲赴上海隨父習練楊家太極拳。吾師年幼聰穎，在其父的嚴格訓練下，無間寒暑、刻苦磨練，少年時打下了堅實的基礎，解放前在其父創辦的永年太極拳社積極協助推廣楊家太極拳。

　　建國後，任上海體育學院武術教練，20世紀60年代初被聘爲武術裁判，多次擔任市級、國家級武術裁判工作；70年代曾受聘於上海同濟大學、化工學院、財經學院等大學，教授楊氏太極拳；1984年與其父參加武漢國際太極拳邀請賽，表演了傳統楊式太極拳、劍、刀、杆（槍），受到了大會的熱烈歡迎和贊賞，新華社記者於上海新民晚報特刊《父子太極》以贊揚。吾師傅聲遠助父義務傳授楊式太極拳數十年，門徒尤重，成就斐然。他先後受聘擔任上海永年太極拳社顧問、上海精武體育總會名譽理事、深圳太極拳研究會顧問、珠海太極拳協會顧問、淮南永年太極拳社名譽社長、邯鄲太極拳友會名譽會長、泰國太極拳會顧問、新加坡楊氏太極拳健康中心顧問總教練、日本東京太極拳社名譽社長、西班牙太極拳學會名譽會長、葡萄牙太極拳學會總教練、印度太極拳學會名譽會長等。

　　1986年，應澳洲友人盛邀移居澳洲，爲傳正宗楊式太極拳於海外，同時遠赴英國、法國、德國、美國、比利時、

瑞士、西班牙、葡萄牙、波蘭、智利、捷克、巴西、紐西蘭、阿根廷、馬西來亞、新加坡、日本、泰國等四十多個國家傳播楊氏太極拳，爲楊氏太極拳傳播海外和人類的健康做出了一定貢獻。1990年，澳洲前總理霍克在柏斯接見並宴請了傳氏父子，贊揚其爲澳洲人民健康做出了貢獻。

吾師傳聲遠，敦厚穩重、樸實無華、虛懷若谷，太極拳造詣頗深，在國內外武術界享有崇高威望，其拳架純正，沉穩中帶有輕靈，拳、劍、刀、杆（槍）、推手無靡不精，大有其父之風範。時令吾師已76歲，秉承父訓，仍不遺餘力，傳正宗楊氏太極拳於海內外。

吾師著有英文版《嫡傳楊家太極拳》、《嫡傳楊家太極劍》，中文英文版《楊氏太極拳精練二十八式》、《二十八式輪椅太極拳》，中文版《嫡傳楊氏太極拳教練法》等著作。此次出版《嫡傳楊家太極拳》、《嫡傳楊家太極劍》、《嫡傳楊家太極刀》，書中圖照分別攝於2003年和2006年，圖照清晰，架式純正，動作規範，詳解拳理拳法，通俗易懂，是一部難得的傳統楊氏太極拳資料，堪稱當今學習楊氏太極拳之範本。受師父之示，爲本書寫跋，弟子受寵若驚，倍感吾師之器重。然本人才疏學淺，草草數語難盡書中之精奧，謹以段文代爲跋。

傳聲遠弟子　楊清波　2006年6月於古趙邯鄲

Postscript Ⅱ

My teacher Fu Shengyuan is the only son of Fu Zhongwen（master of Taijiquan）, Cognation descendant of Yang Style Taijiquan, China Wushu level 8, chairman of World Yongnian Taijiquan Union, chairman of Australia Fu Shengyuan International Taijiquan Institute. He was born in 1931 at Guangfu, Yongnian, Hebei, has went to Shanghai and exercised Taijiquan followed his father since 9 years old. Under stric training from his father, my teacher got a firm base. He actively promoted Yang Style Taijiquan at Yongnian Taijiquan League before liberation.

After PRC established, He held the post of Wushu Coach at Shanghai Physical Training School; at beginning of 60's, he was engaged as Wushu referee, and has atcted as municipality-level, state-level Wushu referee for many times; in the 70's, he was engaged to teach Taijiquan at Shanghai Tongji University, Shanghai University of Economics and Finance, South China University of Technology and other universities; in 1984, in company with his father, he took part in Wuhan International Taijiquan Invitation Competition, and performed traditional Yang Style Taijiquan, Jian（sword）, Dao（knift）, Gan（pole）with his father,was warmly welcomed by the organizer and audience, Xinmin Evening Newspaper has published "Taiji father & Son" to praise them. My teacher has helped his father volunteered to teach Yang Style Taijiquan for decade years, taught lots of disciples, gained great achievements. He has successively acted adviser of Shanghai Yongnian Taijiquan League; honor director of Shanghai Jingwu Gym General Society; adviser of Shenzhen Taiji Research Society; adviser of Zhuhai Taijiquan Association; honor president of Huainan Yongnian Taijiquan Association; honor chief of Handan

Taijiquan Lover Association; adviser of Thailand Taijiquan Association; adviser and chief coach of Singapore Yang Style Taijiquan Healthy Center; Honor president of Japan Tokyo Taijiquan Society; honor president of Spain Taijiquan Association ; chief coach of Portugal Taijiquan Association, honor president of India Taijiquan Association and others. In year 1986, invited by Australian friend, for teaching authentic Yang Style Taijiquan to overseas, he went aborad to teach boxing. In 1988, his whole family settled down at Perth, Australia. He and his father established Wushu Hall to widely teach disciple Yang Style Taijiquan, and went to England, France, Germany, America, Belgium, Switzerland, Spain, Portugal, Poland, Chile, Czechoslovakia, Brazil, New Zealand, Argentina, Malaysia, Singapore, Japan, Thailand, altogether more than 40 countries to spread Yang Style Taijiquan, made certain contribution to people's health. In 1990, Australian Former Prime Ministe Mr. Bob Hawke gave an interview to Fu Zhongwen and Fu Shengyuan, praised them for their contribution to health of Australian people.

My teacher Fu Shengyuan is honest and sincere, earnest and simple, extremely open-minded. He has high prestige in domestic and abroad Wushu groups; he is expert in Taijiquan (boxing) , Jian (sword) , Dao (knife) , Gan (pole) , Tuishou. His boxing posture is pure and authentic, combined calm with nimble together. Now my teacher has already 77 years old, he still obeyed orders from his father, spared no efforts to teach Yang Style Taijiquan at home and abroad. He has written English version Direct-Line Yang Style Taijiquan, Direct-Line Yang Style Taijiquan (sword) ; Chinese and English version Proficiency in 28 Postures of Yang Style Taijiquan, Play 28 Postures of Taijiquan on Wheelchair and Chinese version Exercise Method of Direct-Line Yang Style Taijiquan. This time, he pulished proficiency in 28 Postures of Yang Style Taijiquan, Direct-Line Yang

Style Taijiquan（Sword）, Direct-Line Yang Style Taijidao（knife）（Color version in Chinese and English）, the photos in the books are took in 2003 and 2006. The book has clear photos, standard postures, detail explanation on boxing principle, easy to understand, is a rare information on traditional Yang Style Taijiquan, it can be exercising model for Yang Style Taijiquan. Been instructed to write the Postscipt by my teacher, I was surprised at the unexpected honor. So I tried my best to write down the postrcsipt hereby.

Writer: Disciple of Fu Shengyuan Yang Qingbo

Jun. 2006 at Handan

傅聲遠先生聯絡地址：

澳洲地址：813, ROWLEY ROAD, FORRESDALE, 6112, PERTH, W. Australia

澳洲電話：61-8-93970610　13901649686

上海地址：200081　上海市虹口區四達路58弄8號203

上海電話：（021）65751686

導引養生功

 1 疏筋壯骨功＋VCD　定價350元

 2 導引保健功＋VCD　定價350元

 3 頤身九段錦＋VCD　定價350元

 4 九九還童功＋VCD　定價350元

 5 舒心平血功＋VCD　定價350元

 6 益氣養肺功＋VCD　定價350元

 7 養生太極扇＋VCD　定價350元

 8 養生太極棒＋VCD　定價350元

 9 導引養生形體詩韻＋VCD　定價350元

 10 四十九式經絡動功＋VCD　定價350元

張廣德養生著作　每冊定價350元

全系列為彩色圖解附教學光碟

輕鬆學武術

 1 二十四式太極拳＋VCD　定價250元

 2 四十二式太極拳＋VCD　定價250元

 3 八式十六式太極拳＋VCD　定價250元

 4 三十二式太極劍＋VCD　定價250元

 5 四十二式太極劍＋VCD　定價250元

 6 二十八式木蘭拳＋VCD　定價250元

 7 三十八式木蘭扇＋VCD　定價250元

8 四十八式太極劍＋VCD　定價250元

彩色圖解太極武術

1 太極功夫扇
定價220元

2 武當太極劍
定價220元

3 楊式太極劍56式
定價220元

4 楊式太極刀
定價220元

5 二十四式太極拳+VCD
定價350元

6 三十二式太極劍+VCD
定價350元

7 四十二式太極劍+VCD
定價350元

8 四十二式太極拳+VCD
定價350元

9 楊式十八式太極劍拳
定價350元

10 楊氏二十八式太極拳+VCD
定價350元

11 楊式太極拳四十式+VCD
定價350元

12 陳式太極拳五十六式+VCD
定價350元

13 吳式太極拳五十六式+VCD
定價350元

14 精簡陳式太極拳八十六式
定價220元

15 精簡吳式太極拳三十六式·拳架·推手
定價220元

16 夕陽美功夫扇
定價220元

17 綜合四十八式太極拳+VCD
定價350元

18 三十二式太極拳 四段
定價220元

19 楊式三十七式太極拳+VCD
定價350元

20 楊氏五十一式太極劍+VCD
定價350元

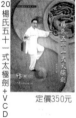

21 嫡傳楊家太極拳精練二十八式
定價220元

22 嫡傳楊家太極劍五十一式
定價220元

太極跤

1 太極防身術

定價300元

2 擒拿術

定價280元

3 中國式摔角

定價350元

簡化太極拳

1 陳式太極拳十三式

定價200元

2 楊式太極拳十三式

定價200元

3 吳式太極拳十三式

定價200元

4 武式太極拳十三式

定價200元

5 孫式太極拳十三式

定價200元

6 趙堡太極拳十三式

定價200元

原地太極拳

1 原地綜合太極二十四式

定價220元

2 原地活步太極四十二式

定價200元

3 原地簡化太極拳二十四式

定價200元

4 原地太極拳十二式

定價200元

5 原地青少年太極拳二十二式

定價220元

6 原地兒童太極拳十捶十六式

定價180元

健康加油站

1 糖尿病預防與治療
定價200元

2 胃部機能與強健
定價180元

3 不孕症治療
定價200元

4 簡易醫學急救法
定價200元

5 肥胖健康診療
定價200元

6 肝功能健康診療
定價200元

7 高血壓健康診療
定價200元

8 高血糖值健康診療
定價200元

9 尿酸值健康診療
定價200元

10 膽固醇中性脂肪健康診療
定價200元

11 痛風劇痛消除法
定價180元

12 三溫暖健康法
定價180元

13 手‧腳‧御秀里安摩
定價180元

14 B型肝炎預防與治療
定價180元

15 吃得更漂亮、健康
定價180元

16 茶使您更健康
定價180元

17 圖解常見疾病運動療法
定價180元

18 科學健身改變亞健康
定價180元

19 簡易萬病自療保健
定價220元

20 王朝秘藥媚酒
定價180元

21 立見實效保健操
定價180元

22 越吃越幸福
定價200元

23 荷爾蒙與健康
定價180元

24 越吃越長壽
定價200元

25 自我保健鍛鍊
定價180元

26 斷食促進健康
定價180元

27 蔬菜健康法
定價200元

28 水果健康法
定價200元

運動精進叢書

1 怎樣跑得快

定價200元

2 怎樣投得遠

定價180元

3 怎樣跳得遠

定價180元

4 怎樣跳得高

定價180元

5 高爾夫揮桿原理

定價220元

6 網球技巧圖解

定價220元

7 排球技巧圖解

定價230元

8 沙灘排球技巧圖解

定價230元

9 撞球技巧圖解

定價230元

10 籃球技巧圖解

定價220元

11 足球技巧圖解

定價230元

12 羽毛球技巧圖解

定價220元

13 乒乓球技巧圖解

定價220元

14 曲線球與飛碟球

定價300元

15 街頭花式籃球

定價280元

16 精彩高爾夫

定價330元

17 巴西青少年足球訓練方法300例

定價230元

18 籃球個人技術全圖解＋VCD

定價300元

19 門球（槌球）入門與提升180問

定價230元

大展好書　好書大展

品嘗好書　冠群可期